YOM KIPPUR
A
FAMILY
SERVICE

BY JUDITH Z. ABRAMS
ILLUMINATED BY KATHERINE JANUS KAHN

KAR-BEN COPIES, INC.   ROCKVILLE, MD

ACKNOWLEDGEMENTS

My greatest thanks to Judye Groner and Madeline Wikler for giving me the opportunity to write these services, and the guidance to make them what they are.

Thanks to Rabbi Oscar Groner for his insights and inspirations.

Thanks to Fran Goldman for the gift of music and to Katherine Kahn for the gift of beauty.

Thanks to Marcia Russell for her insights and help.

Thanks to Congregation Ner Shalom for supporting this work.

Thanks to my husband Steven and my son Michael for their love and patience.

Published by KAR-BEN Publishing, Inc. 1-800-4-KARBEN
A division of Lerner Publishing Group
241 First Avenue North
Minneapolis, MN 55401 U.S.A.

Manufactured in the United States of America
1 2 3 4 5 6 – JR – 07 06 05 04 03 02

DAY
OF
ATONEMENT

TURNING

Turning, turning, turning,
On this holy day.
Turning, turning, turning,
Each in our own way.

We turn to God—that's Tefillah,
We turn to others—Teshuvah,
We turn to those who need our care,
That's called Tzedakah.

TODAY is Yom Kippur, the Day of Atonement.
Ten days ago, on Rosh Hashanah, we welcomed the
new year and promised to do better this year.

We promised to do tefillah, teshuvah, and tzedakah.

We promised to pray, to make up for our mistakes,
and to share.

In the ten days since Rosh Hashanah, we have tried to make up with the people we hurt during the last year.

TODAY, we do something different.
TODAY, we apologize to God.

How can we apologize to God?

We apologize the same way we do with our friends and family—with tefillah, teshuvah, and tzedakah.

תפלה · תשובה · צדקה

FASTING

TODAY, we fast.
We do not eat or drink.
We do not go to work or to parties.
Today, we come to synagogue.
Today, we pray.

Fasting helps us think about tefillah, teshuvah, and tzedakah. Fasting also hurts. And when we hurt, we begin to understand how others feel when they hurt.

תכלה

TEFILLAH

TEFILLAH

We begin with tefillah, prayer. Prayer is our way of talking to God.

We pray when we are amazed, or pleased, or scared.

We pray when something special happens: when we see a rainbow, or trees flowering in the spring, or when we celebrate a holiday.

And we have prayers that say "thank you" for things that happen every day: when the sun rises, or we enjoy a meal.

We say many kinds of prayers today.

We rise.

BARECHU

PRAISE GOD

בָּרְכוּ אֶת־יְיָ הַמְבֹרָךְ.

בָּרוּךְ יְיָ הַמְבֹרָךְ לְעוֹלָם וָעֶד.

Barechu et Adonai hamevorach!
Baruch Adonai hamevorach le'olam va'ed!

Bless Adonai Who is to be blessed!
Blessed is Adonai forever!

We sit down.

YOTZER OR

CREATOR

When we look around and see the world God has made for us, we feel grateful.

Thank You, God, for giving us sight and light to see this beautiful world.

בָּרוּךְ אַתָּה יְיָ יוֹצֵר הַמְּאוֹרוֹת.

Baruch Atah Adonai, yotzer hame'orot.

Blessed are You, Adonai, Who makes light.

AHAVAH RABBAH

GOD'S LOVE

God loves us so much that God gave us a wonderful gift: The Torah. The Torah teaches us who we are and how to live.

Thank You, God, for giving us the gift of Torah.

One way we can show God *our* love is by doing what the Torah tells us to do—by loving God, by loving each other, and by taking care of the world God gave us.

בָּרוּךְ אַתָּה יְיָ הַבּוֹחֵר בְּעמּוֹ יִשְׂרָאֵל בְּאַהֲבָה.

Baruch Atah Adonai, habocher b'amo Yisrael b'ahavah.

Blessed are You, Adonai, Who loves the Jewish People.

TEFILLAH

שְׁמַע יִשְׂרָאֵל יְיָ אֱלֹהֵינוּ יְיָ אֶחָד

Shema Yisrael Adonai Eloheinu Adonai Echad.

Listen O Israel, Adonai is our God, Adonai Alone.

בָּרוּךְ שֵׁם כְּבוֹד מַלְכוּתוֹ לְעוֹלָם וָעֶד.

Baruch shem k'vod malchuto l'olam va'ed.

Blessed is God Who rules forever.

וְאָהַבְתָּ אֵת יְיָ אֱלֹהֶיךָ בְּכָל־לְבָבְךָ
וּבְכָל־נַפְשְׁךָ וּבְכָל־מְאֹדֶךָ.

V'ahavta et Adonai Elohecha b'chol l'vavcha,
uv'chol nafshecha uv'chol m'odecha.

You should love Adonai, your God,
  with all your heart
  with all your soul
  and with all your might

AVOT

God shows us love in yet another way. God made us part of a big family, the Jewish people. This family has lasted thousands of years.

| ABRAHAM SARAH | ISAAC REBECCA | JACOB RACHEL • LEAH |

We rise.

Many people in our family have done things we can be proud of. They were brave and faithful, kind and patient.

בָּרוּךְ אַתָּה יְיָ אֱלֹהֵינוּ, אֱלֹהֵי אַבְרָהָם, אֱלֹהֵי
יִצְחָק, וֵאלֹהֵי יַעֲקֹב. אֱלֹהֵי שָׂרָה, אֱלֹהֵי רִבְקָה,
אֱלֹהֵי רָחֵל וֵאלֹהֵי לֵאָה.

Baruch Atah Adonai Eloheinu, Elohei Avraham, Elohei Yitzchak, velohei Ya'akov, Elohei Sarah, Elohei Rivka, Elohei Rachel, velohei Leah.

Blessed are You, Adonai our God, God of Abraham, Isaac, and Jacob; God of Sarah, Rebecca, Rachel and Leah. Thank You for making us a part of the Jewish people.

We sit down.

YIZKOR

Today, on Yom Kippur, we remember people in our family who lived long ago, and ones who lived with us until just a while ago.

We miss them and wish they were still with us.

Even though they are gone, we can still love them, talk to them, and tell them we are sorry if we hurt them.

God is part of our big family, too. Having God in our family is like having an extra parent who loves us, teaches us, and helps us.

TEFILLAH

We open the Ark and rise.

AVINU MALKENU *hear our voice!*

AVINU MALKENU *make an end to sickness, war, and hunger!*

AVINU MALKENU *may this new year be a good one!*

AVINU MALKENU *fill our hands with Your blessings!*

AVINU MALKENU, be gracious to us and answer us, for we have not done enough good deeds. Please love us, be generous with us, and help us.

AVINU MALKENU

אָבִינוּ מַלְכֵּנוּ חָנֵּנוּ וַעֲנֵנוּ כִּי אֵין

בָּנוּ מַעֲשִׂים עֲשֵׂה עִמָּנוּ צְדָקָה

וָחֶסֶד וְהוֹשִׁיעֵנוּ:

*Avinu Malkenu chanenu va'anenu
Ki ein banu ma'asim.
Aseh imanu tzedakah vachesed, v'hoshi'enu.*

One of the ways parents show love for their children is by asking for God's blessing on them.

MAY GOD BLESS YOU

יְבָרֶכְךָ יְיָ וְיִשְׁמְרֶךָ. יָאֵר יְיָ פָּנָיו אֵלֶיךָ וִיחֻנֶּךָּ.

יִשָּׂא יְיָ פָּנָיו אֵלֶיךָ וְיָשֵׂם לְךָ שָׁלוֹם.

*Y'vareche'cha Adonai v'yishmerecha.
Ya'er Adonai panav elecha vichuneka.
Yisa Adonai panav elecha, v'yasem l'cha shalom.*

May God bless you and keep you.
May God watch over you in kindness.
May God grant you a life of good health,
joy, and peace.

We sit down.

When we are with our families, we may act differently at different times.

Sometimes we seem like grownups, busy and serious.

Sometimes we seem like little children, playful and silly.

Even when we act in different ways, we are still the same person. We are just showing a different side of ourselves.

ME

GOD AND ME

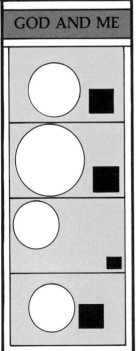

It can be the same with God.

Sometimes God seems like a friend.

Sometimes God seems like a parent.

Sometimes God feels far away.

Sometimes God feels very close.

These are all different sides of God. The more of God we get to know, the closer to God we can feel.

TEFILLAH

KI ANU AMECHA

כִּי אָנוּ עַמֶּךָ וְאַתָּה אֱלֹהֵינוּ. אָנוּ בָנֶיךָ וְאַתָּה אָבִינוּ.

אָנוּ נַחֲלָתֶךָ וְאַתָּה גוֹרָלֵנוּ. אָנוּ כַרְמֶךָ וְאַתָּה נוֹטְרֵנוּ.

אָנוּ עַמֶּךָ וְאַתָּה מַלְכֵּנוּ. אָנוּ רַעְיָתֶךָ וְאַתָּה דוֹדֵנוּ.

Ki anu amecha, v'atah Eloheinu.
Anu vanecha, v'atah avinu,
Anu nachlatecha, v'atah goralenu.
Anu charmecha, v'atah notrenu.
Anu amecha, v'atah malkenu.
Anu rayatecha, v'atah dodenu.

We are Your people, and You are our God.
We are Your children, and You are our parent.
We are your future, and You are our fate.
We are Your responsibility, and You are our leader.
We are Your people, and You are our ruler.
We are your companion, and You are our friend.

TURNING

Turning, turning, turning,
On this holy day.
Turning, turning, turning,
Each in our own way.

We turn to God—that's Tefillah,
We turn to others—Teshuvah,
We turn to those who need our care,
That's called Tzedakah.

Now, let us turn to God by doing Teshuvah.

תשובה

TESHUVAH

TESHUVAH

Some of the prayers we say today have a secret message in them. Each letter in the word Teshuvah can stand for a good deed or a bad deed. As we read this prayer, let us think back over what we did during the last year.

We   **T**   Told the truth

We ran   **E**   Errands

We   **S**   Shared

We   **H**   Helped

We   **U**   Understood

We   **V**   Volunteered

We   **A**   Acted properly

We   **H**   Hugged

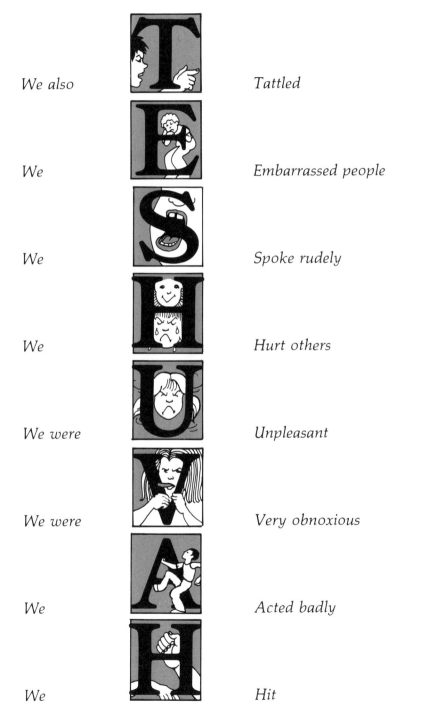

We also	**T**	*Tattled*
We	**E**	*Embarrassed people*
We	**S**	*Spoke rudely*
We	**H**	*Hurt others*
We were	**U**	*Unpleasant*
We were	**V**	*Very obnoxious*
We	**A**	*Acted badly*
We	**H**	*Hit*

TESHUVAH

Let us think to ourselves about the good and bad things we have done.

We pray silently.

We feel proud of many things we did last year.

We feel ashamed of other things we did last year.

God, please help us make up for our mistakes, today, and all year long.

Please help us say we are sorry. Please help us improve our behavior.

God, please forgive us when we say we are sorry.

We are ready to forgive those who have hurt us. We pray others will forgive us when we say we are sorry.

I'M SORRY

> ## V'AL KULAM
>
> וְעַל כֻּלָּם, אֱלוֹהַּ סְלִיחוֹת,
>
> סְלַח־לָנוּ, מְחַל־לָנוּ, כַּפֶּר־ לָנוּ!
>
> *V'al kulam Eloha selichot*
> *s'lach lanu, m'chal lanu, kaper lanu.*

*And for all the things we have done wrong,
forgive us, pardon us, grant us atonement.*

WHY IS IT SO HARD TO BE GOOD?

Each of us is free to choose to do right or wrong. We can think of it this way: inside each of us is a Yetzer Hara, a will to do wrong, and a Yetzer Tov, a will to do right.

We cannot get rid of our Yetzer Hara. It will always be with us. It can even help...but *only* if our Yetzer Tov controls it. Each of us has to decide whom to put in charge of our life: our Yetzer Tov or our Yetzer Hara.

YETZER HARA

My Yetzer Hara, my Yetzer Hara
My urge to do what's wrong,
My Yetzer Hara, my Yetzer Hara
Sometimes it seems so strong.

My Yetzer Hara, my Yetzer Hara
It always will be here.
But Yetzer Hara, ah, Yetzer Hara
There's something that you fear.

My Yetzer Tov, my Yetzer Tov
My urge to do what's good.
My Yetzer Tov, my Yetzer Tov
Helps me act as I should.

My Yetzer Tov, my Yetzer Tov
When you're helping me,
My Yetzer Tov, my Yetzer Tov
A hero's what I'll be! (2)

READING THE TORAH

The Torah teaches us how we can do Teshuvah.

We rise as we take the Torah from the Ark.

כִּי מִצִּיּוֹן תֵּצֵא תוֹרָה וּדְבַר־יְיָ מִירוּשָׁלָיִם.

Ki Mitzion tetzei Torah, u'dvar Adonai Mirushalayim.

The Torah will come from Zion, and God's word
from Jerusalem.

שְׁמַע יִשְׂרָאֵל יְיָ אֱלֹהֵינוּ יְיָ אֶחָד

Shema Yisrael Adonai Eloheinu Adonai Echad.

Listen O Israel, Adonai is our God, Adonai Alone.

God is one. Holy and awesome is God's name.

We sit down.

בָּרְכוּ אֶת יְיָ הַמְבֹרָךְ!

בָּרוּךְ יְיָ הַמְבוֹרָךְ לְעוֹלָם וָעֶד!

בָּרוּךְ אַתָּה יְיָ אֱלֹהֵינוּ מֶלֶךְ הָעוֹלָם, אֲשֶׁר בָּחַר־

בָּנוּ מִכָּל־הָעַמִּים וְנָתַן־לָנוּ אֶת־תּוֹרָתוֹ.

בָּרוּךְ אַתָּה יְיָ, נוֹתֵן הַתּוֹרָה.

Barechu et Adonai hamevorach!
Baruch Adonai hamevorach l'olam va'ed!
Baruch Atah Adonai, Eloheinu Melech ha'olam, asher bachar
banu mikol ha'amim, venatan lanu et Torato.
Baruch Atah Adonai, Noten Hatorah.

18

TORAH SERVICE

Bless Adonai Who is to be blessed!

Blessed is Adonai forever!

Blessed are You, Adonai our God, Ruler of the world, Who chose us and gave us the Torah.

Blessed are You, Adonai, Giver of Torah.

TORAH READING

LEVITICUS 23: 26-28

וַיְדַבֵּר יהוה אֶל־מֹשֶׁה לֵּאמֹר: אַךְ בֶּעָשׂוֹר לַחֹדֶשׁ הַשְּׁבִיעִי הַזֶּה יוֹם הַכִּפֻּרִים הוּא מִקְרָא־קֹדֶשׁ יִהְיֶה לָכֶם וְעִנִּיתֶם אֶת־נַפְשֹׁתֵיכֶם וְהִקְרַבְתֶּם אִשֶּׁה לַיהוה: וְכָל־מְלָאכָה לֹא תַעֲשׂוּ בְּעֶצֶם הַיּוֹם הַזֶּה כִּי יוֹם כִּפֻּרִים הוּא לְכַפֵּר עֲלֵיכֶם לִפְנֵי יהוה אֱלֹהֵיכֶם:

GOD SAID to Moses, "On the tenth day of the seventh month of the year, you will have a Day of Atonement. On this day you will not eat. You will not work. You will just think about what you have done wrong and how you can make it right."

TORAH

BLESSING

בָּרוּךְ אַתָּה יְיָ אֱלֹהֵינוּ מֶלֶךְ הָעוֹלָם, אֲשֶׁר נָתַן־לָנוּ תּוֹרַת אֱמֶת וְחַיֵּי עוֹלָם נָטַע בְּתוֹכֵנוּ. בָּרוּךְ אַתָּה יְיָ, נוֹתֵן הַתּוֹרָה.

Baruch Atah Adonai, Eloheinu melech ha'olam, asher natan lanu Torat emet, vechayei olam nata b'tochenu.
Baruch Atah Adonai, Noten Hatorah.

Blessed are You, Adonai Our God, Ruler of the World, Who gave us the Torah and gave us eternal life. Blessed are You, Adonai, Giver of Torah.

HAFTORAH READING

Today, we read the story of Jonah. Jonah was a prophet, like Elijah. But unlike Elijah, who looked for God everywhere, Jonah tried to hide from God.

Once, God spoke to Jonah and said, "Jonah, go to the city of Nineveh and tell the people they have done evil. Tell them God said to behave better, or they will be punished." But Jonah didn't want to go. And he didn't want to talk to God anymore.

Jonah went down to the harbor and got on a ship going to the city of Tarshish, so he could hide from God. But God found him on the ship. God brought a big rainstorm on the sea. The storm was so strong that the ship began to break apart. Jonah knew that God had brought the storm because he had tried to hide from God. He told the sailors on board to throw him into the sea. As soon as they did, the storm stopped.

While Jonah floated in the water, God caused a huge fish to swallow him up. Jonah lived in the belly of the fish for three days and three nights. He had a lot of time to think and to pray. Jonah realized that trying to run away was wrong. God heard Jonah's thoughts and caused the fish to let Jonah go. Once again God told Jonah to go to Nineveh to warn the people. This time Jonah went, and the people listened.

They did teshuvah. They stopped their evil ways. They apologized to others they had hurt. And they began to behave better. So God did not punish the people of Nineveh. This made Jonah angry. He thought that if people do something wrong, they ought to be punished. But that is not what God wanted. God wanted the people to do teshuvah, to make up for their mistakes. God did not want to punish the people of Nineveh, and God does not want to punish us, either. God would rather have us do teshuvah. God wants to be able to forgive us.

TESHUVAH

We return the Torah to the Ark.

ETZ CHAIM

עֵץ־חַיִּים הִיא לַמַּחֲזִיקִים בָּהּ
וְתוֹמְכֶיהָ מְאֻשָּׁר.
דְּרָכֶיהָ דַרְכֵי־נֹעַם וְכָל־נְתִיבוֹתֶיהָ שָׁלוֹם

Etz chayim hi, l'machazikim bah.
Vetom'cheha me'ushar.
Deracheha, darchei no'am,
Vechol netivoteha shalom.

The Torah is a tree of life
When we hold it close.
Its ways are pleasant and peaceful.

We close the Ark.

Now let us turn to God through tzedakah, by caring and sharing.

TURNING

Turning, turning, turning,
On this holy day.
Turning, turning, turning,
Each in our own way.

We turn to God—that's Tefillah,
We turn to others—Teshuvah,
We turn to those who need our care,
That's called Tzedakah.

צְדָקָה

TZEDAKAH

TZEDAKAH

Giving tzedakah means sharing what you have with someone who needs it.

We can share our food,

our clothes,

our toys,

and our money.

We can also share our time and our friendship.

We can honor our parents.

We can help others when they're sad or sick.

We can be friendly.

We pray that the time comes when all people will share, and everybody will have enough of what they need.

We rise.

ALEINU

עָלֵינוּ לְשַׁבֵּחַ לַאֲדוֹן הַכֹּל לָתֵת גְּדֻלָּה לְיוֹצֵר בְּרֵאשִׁית

וַאֲנַחְנוּ כּוֹרְעִים וּמִשְׁתַּחֲוִים וּמוֹדִים

לִפְנֵי מֶלֶךְ מַלְכֵי הַמְּלָכִים הַקָּדוֹשׁ בָּרוּךְ הוּא.

Aleinu leshabe'ach la'adon hakol. Latet gedulah l'yotzer bereshit.
Va'anachnu kor'im u'mishtachavim u'modim, Lifnei melech malchei hamelachim, Hakadosh baruch Hu.

Let us praise God, Who created this world and created us. Together, we will work for the day when the whole world is one and at peace.

We sit down.

TZEDAKAH

TODAY, we promise to do better.

We promise to pray.

We promise to make up for our mistakes.

We promise to share.

May this next year be a sweet one!

TURNING

Turning, turning, turning,
On this holy day.
Turning, turning, turning,
Each in our own way.

We turn to God—that's Tefillah,
We turn to others—Teshuvah,
We turn to those who need our care,
That's called Tzedakah.

We blow the shofar.

BLOWING THE SHOFAR

TEKIAH GEDOLAH

תְּקִיעָה גְדוֹלָה

גְּמַר חֲתִימָה טוֹבָה.
G'MAR CHATIMAH TOVAH!
MAY YOU BE SEALED FOR A GOOD YEAR!

IDEAS FOR HOME AND SCHOOL

Today is for apologizing to God, but if we haven't made our apologies to *people* as we ought to have done, asking God to forgive us won't help.

FASTING

Children under 12 years old can give up snacks and treats for the day even though they do not fast. They may also donate the cost of a candy bar or treat to a food bank. Adults may also contribute the cost of the food they would have consumed to a food bank or shelter for the homeless.

YETZER HARA AND YETZER TOV

To graphically demonstrate the balance we need between Yetzer Hara and the Yetzer Tov, attach strings to three helium balloons and weight them down. Take the weight off one balloon, and let it go to the ceiling. This represents the Yetzer Hara when it's out of control. Floating freely may look like fun, but you're totally cut off from everyone, and you can't come back. Shorten the string on the second balloon until it cannot move. This is what life would be like without the Yetzer Hara. There would be no movement at all. We should be like the third balloon: able to move, yet firmly planted in the ground, *using* the Yetzer Hara and keeping it under control.

You may also make puppets out of popsicle sticks or tongue depressors. When a child feels a battle between his/her two "urges", the puppets can facilitate discussion. It's helpful if the two puppets look similar. Then you can point out that sometimes the wrong thing to do can look almost like the right thing to do.

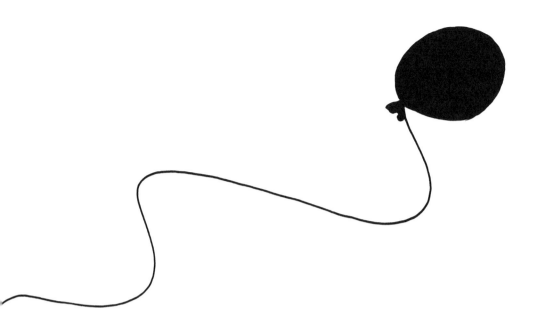

YETZER HARA

The following is a story from the Talmud about the Yetzer Hara.

One day, long ago, the rabbis caught the Grand-daddy Yetzer Hara, and they locked him up for three days. The rabbis thought everything would be wonderful without the Evil Urge around. There would be no fights, no stealing, and no lying. And they were right. But there were also no houses built and no chickens raised. Nothing got done.

The rabbis realized that we *need* the Yetzer Hara. It gives us the drive to succeed, and build, and conquer the world. If we let the Yetzer Hara have complete control, it will go too far. That's why our Yetzer Tov, our Good Urge, has to be stronger than our Yetzer Hara.

So the rabbis, sighing, sent the Yetzer Hara back out into the world, together with the Yetzer Tov. And they roam the world together to this very day.

TURNING

Words by Judith Z. Abrams
Music by Frances T. Goldman

Moderate tempo

Turn-ing turn-ing turn-ing on this ho-ly day.

Turn-ing turn-ing turn-ing each in our own way. We

turn to God, that's T'fi - lah. We turn to oth - ers: T'shu - vah. We

turn to those who need our care. That's called Tz'da - kah. We

turn to those who need our care. That's called Tz'da - kah.

Turn-ing turn-ing turn-ing on this ho-ly day.

Turn-ing turn-ing turn-ing each in our own way.

each in our own way.

YETZER HARA

Moderately fast; with spirit

Words by Judith Z. Abrams
Music by Frances T. Goldman

My Ye - tzer Ha - ra, my Ye - tzer Ha - ra, my urge to do what's wrong. My Ye - tzer ha - ra, my Ye - tzer ha - ra. Some - times it seems so strong. my be! A he - ro's what I'll be.

2.

My Yetzer Hara, my Yetzer Hara
It always will be here.
But Yetzer Hara, ah, Yetzer Hara
There's something that you fear.

3.

My Yetzer Tov, my Yetzer Tov
My urge to do what's good.
My Yetzer Tov, my Yetzer Tov
Helps me act as I should.

4.

My Yetzer Tov, my Yetzer Tov
When you're helping me,
My Yetzer Tov, my Yetzer Tov
A hero's what I'll be! (2)

JUDITH Z. ABRAMS, a graduate of Oberlin College, was ordained at the Hebrew Union College-Jewish Institute of Religion in 1985. She has served congregations in Ohio, Illinois, and Texas, and is currently rabbi of Congregation Ner Shalom in Woodbridge, VA. She is the author of books on the Talmud for adults.

KATHERINE JANUS KAHN, an illustrator, calligrapher, and sculptor, studied Fine Arts at the Bezalel School in Jerusalem, and the University of Iowa. She has illustrated an impressive list of Jewish books for children, including *The Yanov Torah, The Odd Potato, A Family Haggadah,* and a series of toddler board books for Kar-Ben. She lives in Wheaton, MD.

FRANCES T. GOLDMAN has a B.A. in voice and an M.A. in speech and theater from the College Conservatory of Music of the University of Cincinnati. She is the cantor and music director at Congregation Beth Ahabah in Richmond, VA. In addition to writing original music for the High Holiday Services, she produced a companion tape, *Songs for the High Holidays.*

KAR-BEN COPIES, INC., publishes over 80 books and tapes of Jewish interest for young children and their families.

This book is part of a series of High Holiday Family services, which includes:

> **Selichot — A Family Service**
> **Rosh Hashanah — A Family Service**
> **Yom Kippur — A Family Service**
> and a companion cassette tape, **Songs for the High Holidays**

Available at selected bookstores or from Kar-Ben Copies at 1-800-4-KARBEN